Speaking With Other Tongues

Speaking With Other Tongues

SIGN OR GIFT

WHICH?

By

T. J. McCROSSAN, B.A., B.D.

CHRISTIAN PUBLICATIONS, INC.
Harrisburg, Pa.

Contents

Chapter 1

Are Tongues For Today?

Today hundreds of God's saints really speak with other tongues when baptized or filled with the Holy Ghost, just as the hundred and twenty Galilæans spake on the day of Pentecost.

The writer, like scores of other theological students, was taught that the Holy Spirit never took possession of people's tongues today, and made them praise God in another language. This only happened in Apostolic times, our professors told us. However, we now know that these honored teachers were mistaken.

One night, after a great evangelistic meeting where scores had been saved, we saw the evangelist himself overcome by the power of God while in prayer, and we heard him speak Chinese. We recognized the language because we had so often heard it spoken; but God, in His goodness, had a Christian Alliance missionary standing by our side, a man we knew, trusted and loved. He had been a Chinese missionary for over eighteen years. He whispered to us, "He is praising God in the very Chinese dialect I preach in; he is speaking it perfectly, and oh, how he is praising the Lord Jesus." He then interpreted sentence after sentence to us. It was indeed wonderful, as we both knew that the evangelist was absolutely ignorant of the Chinese language.

On another occasion we heard an American woman, when filled with the Holy Ghost, praise God in Norwegian. We knew it was either Norwegian or Swedish, for we had heard these languages so frequently in Minneapolis. However our gracious Lord had a Norwegian gentleman standing by our side, who said, "Brother McCrossan, I know this woman. She is an American and utterly ignorant of my language (Norwegian), and yet she is speaking it perfectly, and oh, sir, I have never heard any one praise the Lord Jesus as she is doing."

On another occasion we heard a person praising the Lord Jesus in perfect French, one who was utterly ignorant of that language. We have frequently heard young people both speak and sing in other tongues, as the Spirit gave them utterance; singing with a voice so vastly superior to their own natural voice, that there was no comparison. No interpreter was present on these occasions, and yet we felt certain these were genuine languages (having studied five different languages), and we knew from the tone, the facial expression and the marvelous joy that it was the work of the Holy Spirit. There was something about it so sweet, so attractive, so helpful, something that actually drew one into the very presence of God, and made one feel that which he ought to be beating beneath that which he really was.

Just here let us say, that we have also heard many good people speak with other tongues when we felt absolutely sure that the Holy Spirit had nothing whatever to do with the speaking; but we shall deal with this matter later.

Yes, hundreds today are really speaking with other tongues when baptized or filled with the Holy Ghost, just as on the day of Pentecost, and this is only one more sure sign of the soon-coming of our blessed Lord. Did not Peter assure us that Pentecost was only a sample of what Joel predicted would happen in the last days? Acts 2:16, "But this is that which was spoken by the prophet Joel; (17) And it shall come to pass in the last days, saith God, I will pour out of my Spirit upon all flesh: and your sons and your daughters shall prophesy [preach or teach in public], and your young men shall see visions, and your old men shall dream dreams: (18) And upon my male servants and upon my female servants [literal translation] I will pour out in those days of my Spirit; and they shall prophesy [prophēteusousin—preach or teach publicly]."

God is now again pouring out His Spirit upon both His male and female servants, and when He says His female servants in the last days shall preach and expound Scripture publicly, let some of us beware how we condemn "women pastors," who are Spirit-filled.

Today so many are "speaking with other tongues" when baptized or filled with the Holy

11

Ghost, that hundreds of sincere and earnest saints are conscientiously teaching that all truly baptized persons must so speak, as this is the one and only sure Bible evidence.

But what says the Word on this most important subject? Surely, surely God has not left His people in the dark regarding such a vital truth as this. A close study of the original Greek text will assuredly give us light.

Chapter 2

Studying the Scriptures

Tongue Passages Examined

Here let us examine Acts 2:4, Acts 10:44-46, and Acts 19:6 and see what the Bible really teaches regarding "speaking with other tongues."

In Acts 1:5, Christ says, "But ye shall be baptized with the Holy Ghost not many days hence." Then we read (Acts 2:4), "And they were all filled with the Holy Ghost, and began to speak with other tongues, as the Spirit gave them utterance."

(1) *"And they were all filled with the Holy Ghost."* The Greek word here for "were filled" is "eplēsthēsan," 1 Aorist passive, third person plural of "pimplēmi" I fill.

Now the Aorist tense always denotes that something took place and was completed in the past. Then "eplēthēsan" (were filled), being the Aorist tense, assures us as plainly as language can possibly do, that their baptism with the Holy Ghost was made a past action there and then.

(2) "......and began to speak with other tongues as the Spirit gave to them to utter forth" (literal translation). The word for "gave" here in the Greek text is "edidou," the third person singular, Imperfect tense of "didōmi" (I give).

Now the Imperfect tense in Greek has an entirely different meaning from the Aorist. It always designates continued or repeated past action. Had this speaking with other tongues only happened once, when the hundred and twenty were baptized, as God's sign or seal of the genuine baptism, then most assuredly the Greek word for "gave" here would have been "edōke" (third person singular, 1 Aorist of didōmi—I give) and not "edidou," the Imperfect tense. The use of the Aorist here (edōke) would have told us positively that the Holy Spirit just gave to them to utter forth in another tongue on that occasion: but the use of the Imperfect tense (edidou) proves to us beyond the shadow of a doubt, that the Holy Spirit gave them to utter forth in other tongues then, and continued to do so, repeating this experience over and over again. *If Peter himself were to come back to earth he could not state this fact any more clearly than the Greek text here states it by using the Aorist tense regarding the being filled with the Spirit, and the Imperfect tense regarding the Spirit giving them to utter forth in other tongues.*

This proves most conclusively that "the speaking with other tongues" at Pentecost was "the gift of tongues," and not something that just occurred at that time as the sign or seal of their baptism. No person, therefore, is ever baptized according to Acts 2:4 unless this "speaking with other tongues" is a continued and repeated experience. We would not say that persons who speak in tongues at their baptism and never again afterwards, were not genuinely baptized with the Holy Ghost; but we do say that they were not baptized according to Acts 2:4, where "the speaking with tongues" was most assuredly something continued, and repeated over and over again, as the use of the Imperfect tense declares.

Just here let us compare Acts 2:4 with Acts 4:31. *Acts 2:4*, "And they were all filled [eplēsthēsan, Aorist tense or past completed action] with the Holy Ghost, and they began to speak with other tongues as the Spirit gave [edidou—Imperfect tense, or continued and repeated action] to them to utter forth." *Acts 4: 31*, "And when they had prayed the place was shaken where they were assembled together; and they were all filled [eplēsthēsan—the same word and the same Aorist tense as Acts 2:4] with the Holy Ghost, and they spake [elaloun, Imperfect tense of laleo, I speak—continued or repeated action] the word of God with boldness."

Note, these persons in Acts 4:31 were just as completely filled with the Holy Ghost as those in Acts 2:4, for the very same Greek word and the very same Aorist tense are used in both cases to designate the completed filling. However, when they were filled, those in Acts 2:4 spoke in other tongues, and continued to do so,

15

as the Spirit gave (edidou—Imperfect tense) to them to utter forth; while those in Acts 4:31, after their completed baptism or filling, as brought out by the use of the Aorist tense, spake (elaloun—Imperfect tense) the word of God with boldness, and continued so to do, as the Imperfect tense in Greek always signifies continued or repeated past action. The Saints of Acts 2:4 therefore most assuredly received the gift of tongues after their baptism: those of Acts 4:31 the gift of prophesy. With thousands of unsaved Jews present, who spoke different languages, we can readily see why God gave the gift of tongues at Pentecost.

But what about Acts 10:44-46 and Acts 19:6? Is the same grammatical construction found in these cases also?

Acts 10:44, "While Peter yet spake these words, the Holy Ghost fell upon [epepesen—2 Aorist of epipipto, I fall upon] all them that heard the word. (45) And they of the circumcision which believed, were astonished, as many as came with Peter, because on the Gentiles also was poured out ["ekkechutai"—Perfect Passive, third singular of "ekcheō"] the gift of the Holy Ghost. (46) For they heard [ēkouon—third person plural, Imperfect tense of akouo, I hear] them speaking with tongues and magnifying God" (literal translation).

Note, that the word "epepesen" (fell upon), which here designates the baptism or infilling, is the Aorist tense, which clearly speaks of some action completed in the past. This fact that the baptism with the Holy Ghost was fully completed before the speaking with tongues began, is here made doubly certain by the use of the Perfect tense "ekkechutai" (was poured out). When the Perfect tense is thus used following the Aorist and referring to the very same event, it is to emphasize the fact of the completion of that event at that particular time.

The word "ēkouon" (heard) however, is the Imperfect tense, which most clearly tells us that they heard them speak with tongues and magnify God then, and also at various times afterwards. Remember again that the Imperfect tense in Greek always expresses something continued and repeated in the past; therefore, its use here with regard to hearing them speak with tongues, tells us as plainly as language can express it, that this too was the gift of tongues—something continued and repeated later on—and not something which occurred only at the time of their baptism, as the sign or seal of that baptism. Had they only spoken with tongues at that one particular time, then the Aorist tense ("ēkousan") of this verb "akouō" (I hear) would have been used, and not the Imperfect tense ("ēkouon"), which always designates something continued or repeated in the past.

Let us now examine Acts 19:6: "And when Paul had laid his hands upon them, the Holy Ghost came [ēlthen—third person singular, 2 Aorist of erchomai, I come] upon them, and they spake with tongues and prophesied." "Spake" here is "elaloun," the third person plural, Imperfect tense of "laleō," I speak. The word here for "prophesied" is "proephēteuon," the third person plural, Imperfect tense of prophēteuō—I prophesy.

The word "came" (ēlthen), being the Aorist tense, tells us, as clearly as language can express it, that the filling with the Holy Ghost was completed and made a matter of the past. The words "spake" (elaloun) and "prophesied" (proephēteuon), both being in the Imperfect tense, tell us, as clearly as language can express it, that the speaking with tongues and the prophesying, which followed the completed baptism, were gifts of the Holy Ghost, something to be continued and repeated over and over again.

Conclusions

(1) The use of the Aorist tense in each of these three cases (Acts 2:4, Acts 10:44 and Acts 19:6), when telling of the Spirit filling them or coming upon them, proves most conclusively that "the baptism" was really completed before "the talking with tongues" began.

(2) The use of the Imperfect tense in every single instance where "the speaking with tongues" is mentioned, is absolute proof that in each case this was the gift of tongues following the baptism, something to be continued and repeated again and again in the days yet to come. To any one really versed in the rules of Greek grammar this is so evident that there is absolutely no room for doubt on this question.

Let us here confirm our own conclusions by quoting indisputable authorities. Remember this whole matter is settled when you get a clear understanding of the difference between the meaning of the Aorist and Imperfect tenses in Greek.

(1) *Huddilston,* Essentials of New Testament Greek, p. 55, says, *"The Aorist* is the most common tense in Greek to represent what has taken place." On p. 14, he says, *"The Imperfect* indicative represents an act

as going on in time past—continued, accustomed, or repeated action."

(2) *John Williams White,* First Greek Book, p. 22, says, *"The Aorist* indicative expresses the simple occurrence of an action in time past: *the Imperfect* expresses its continuance."

(3) *Goodell's Greek Grammar* (Paragraph 462), *"The Aorist* indicative presents an action simply as past." (Par. 459) *"The Imperfect* tense presents the action either as continuing, or as being repeated in the past." This is our contention exactly.

(4) *William Edward Jelf* says in his great work, A Grammar of the Greek Language (Par. 401), *"The Aorist* expresses an action simply as past, neither having, like the Perfect, any connection with time present, nor, like the Imperfect, any reference to another action, nor any notion of continuance. *Hence the Aorist is used when any action is to be represented as momentary: and thus is opposed to the Imperfect which designates continuance."* Also in paragraph 398, Jelf says, "By the Imperfect tense an action is represented as going on in time past relatively to another action also in time past. *If this other action is antecedent to the Imperfect it is in the Aorist tense."*

This then explains why in Acts 2:4, Acts 10:44 and Acts 19:6 "the infilling" or "the Spirit coming upon" is expressed by the Aorist. *The baptism or the infilling was antecedent to the speaking with tongues, and because of this it (the infilling or the baptism) is expressed by the Aorist, while "the speaking with tongues," which followed as a gift to be continued and repeated, is expressed by the Imperfect tense, exactly as Jelf explains in paragraph 398 as quoted above.*

(5) *Babbitt's* Greek Grammar (Paragraph 528), *"The Aorist* represents the action as one that simply took place in past time." (Paragraph 526), *"The Imperfect represents an action as going on in past time. Hence the Imperfect expresses a customary past action."*

(6) *Goodwin's Greek Grammar* (Paragraph 1259), "The Aorist denotes a simple past occurrence. Thus 'tauto epoiēse' (Aorist) is simply, he did this; *but 'tauto epoiei' (Imperfect) means he was doing this, or he did this habitually."*

Again remember that while "the filling or the baptism" is always expressed by the Aorist tense, "the speaking with tongues," as we have shown, is always expressed by the Imperfect tense, which Goodwin here declares means to do something habitually; repeated or continued action as Goodell has expressed it above.

(7) *A. T. Robertson,* A Grammar of the Greek New Testament, p. 838, says "Where the Aorist and Imperfect occur side by side, it is to be assumed that the change (from one tense to the other) is made on purpose, and the difference in idea is to be sought." He then shows very clearly that while the Aorist brings out the fact of past action, without any idea of continuance, the Imperfect, just as clearly, expresses the idea of continued, repeated, or habitual action.

(8) See also *Winer's* New Testament Greek Grammar p. 330, Sect. 40, and p. 335, par. 3.

Many other authorities might be quoted, but surely these are sufficient to prove the correctness of our conclusion regarding "the speaking with tongues" in Acts 2:4, Acts 10:46 and Acts 19:6 being "the gift of tongues" and not a sign or seal of the baptism.

To convince every person, at all open to conviction, that this conclusion is correct, let us now examine a few other passages of Scripture to show the exact use of these tenses.

Luke 1:41, "And it came to pass that when Elizabeth heard the salutation of Mary, the babe leaped in her womb; and Elizabeth was filled ["eplēsthē—third person singular, 1 Aorist passive] with the Holy Ghost. (42) And she spake out with a loud voice, and said, Blessed art thou among women," etc. Now Elizabeth only made this speech once and did not continue so to do, so we find the two verbs "spake out" (anephonēsen) and "said" (eipen) in the Aorist tense, which denotes past action without any idea of continuance. Had Elizabeth, after her baptism or infilling, continued again and again, habitually, to say these same words, both these verbs ("spake out" and "said") would have been in the Imperfect tense to denote repeated or continued action.

Again examine Luke 1:67, "And his father Zacharias was filled [eplēsthē—third person singular, 1 Aorist passive] with the Holy Ghost and prophesied [proephēteusen—third person singular, 1 Aorist] saying, Blessed be the Lord God of Israel," etc. Here follows a speech which Zacharias did not continue to repeat; it was completed then and there, so we find this fact set forth by the use of the Aorist tense. He was first filled with the Holy Ghost, as the Aorist tense tells us clearly, and then he prophesied, saying something which he did not continue to repeat, and so the Aorist is again employed to bring out this thought. Had Zacharias continued to prophesy, after having been filled with the Holy Ghost, we would most assuredly have had the

Imperfect tense used to denote continued, repeated or habitual action.

To prove these assertions still further—for we are sincerely seeking to ascertain God's truth on this subject —let us examine Mark 7: 35: "And straightway his ears were opened [diēnoichthēsan—third person plural, 1 Aorist passive of "dianoigō," I open], and the string of his tongue was loosed [eluthē—third person singular, 1 Aorist passive of "luō," I loosen], and he spake [elalei—third person singular, Imperfect tense of "laleō," I speak] plain." Here the momentary or completed past actions were, (1) that his ears were opened, and (2) that the string of his tongue was loosed. These completed past actions are therefore clearly expressed by the use of the Aorist tense. But after that he was cured, he spake plain. Now had Mark just desired to tell us of this miracle without any thought of the man continuing to speak afterwards, the Greek verb here would have been "elalēse" (1 Aorist, third person singular of "laleō"). This would have expressed momentary or completed past action without any reference to continuance. But in place of the Aorist tense here we have the Imperfect, "elalei," which clearly tells us that he began to speak as soon as his tongue was loosed, and continued to speak right along—repeated and continued action.

Again examine Luke 1: 63. "And he [Zacharias, the father of John the Baptist] asked for a writing table, and wrote, saying, His name is John...... (64) And his mouth was opened [aneōchthē—third person singular, 1 Aorist passive of "anoignumi," I open]...... and he spake [elalei—third person singular, Imperfect tense of "laleō," I speak] praising God" (literal translation). His mouth had to be opened before he could possibly speak, so *the fact that his mouth was first opened before anything else happened, is expressed by the Aorist tense.* Then, *after his mouth had been opened by the Lord, he spoke and continued to speak right along. This fact is brought out by putting the word "spake" (elalei) in the Imperfect tense, which always expresses continued, repeated or habitual past action.*

In *Acts 11:18* we have another splendid example of the difference between the Aorist and the Imperfect tenses. Peter was here on trial before the church council for daring to baptize Cornelius and his house. We here read, "And having heard these things, they were silent [hēsuchasan—1 Aorist passive, third person plural of "hēsuchazō," I am silent or still], and they glorified [edoxazon—third person plural, Imperfect of "doxazō," I glorify] God, saying," etc. When they first heard how God had baptized Cornelius and his household, they were so surprised that they could not speak for a few moments, for they never thought God would so bless the despised Gentiles. *Now this fact of their silence, which was only momentary and soon completed, is therefore rightly expressed by the use of the Aorist tense.* But after this completed silence, they began to glorify God for bringing salvation to the Gentiles, and they continued more and more to glorify Him because of this, as the church grew, so we find this word "glorified" (edoxazon) in the Imperfect tense, which always denotes continued, repeated or habitual action.

In *Acts 13:11* we read, "And now, behold, the hand of the Lord is upon thee [Elymas], and thou shalt be blind, not seeing the sun for a season. And immediately there fell on ["epepesen"—third singular, 2 Aorist of "epipiptō," I fall upon] him a mist and a darkness, and he going about [literal translation] sought ["ezētei"—third singular, Imperfect tense of "zēteō," I seek] some one to lead him by the hand." Note, a mist and a darkness fell upon him and made him blind before any one had to lead him about. This past completed action is therefore expressed by the Aorist tense ("epepesen"—the same word and the same tense as in Acts 10:44). Then, after he was blind, he sought some one to lead him around by the hand. The word for sought (ezētei), being the Imperfect tense, assures us that he sought some one to lead him as soon as he became blind, and continued to do so right along— continued, repeated, or habitual action.

Acts 13:45, "But when the Jews saw the multitudes, they were filled ["eplēsthēsan"—third plural, 1 Aorist passive of "pimplēmi," I fill] with envy, and spake against [antelegon—third plural, Imperfect tense of "antilegō," I speak against] those things which were spoken by Paul," etc. Note, they were first filled with envy. This completed past action is expressed by the Aorist tense ("eplēsthēsan—the very same verb and the same tense as in Acts 2:4 and 4:31). Then after they were filled with envy, but not before, they spake against ("antelegon"—Imperfect tense) those things which were spoken by Paul. The Imperfect tense here (antelegon) tells us very plainly that they began then, just as soon as they had been filled with envy, to speak against Paul, and continued so to do from that time on—continued, repeated or habitual action.

Again examine Acts 14:10. Paul here says to a

lame man, crippled in both feet from birth, "Stand upright on thy feet. And he leaped and walked." Here "stand upright" is "anastēthi" (2 Aorist Imperative of "anistēmi"—I stand up). The Aorist Imperative assures us that "the standing up" was made a past or completed action immediately. Then, when he had stood up, he leaped (hēlleto—Imperfect, third singular of hallomai, I leap) and walked (periepatei—Imperfect, third singular of peripateō, I walk). The Aorist Imperative here tells us, as plainly as language can express it, that the man stood on his feet at once, and, when that was accomplished, the Imperfect tenses assure us that he began then to leap and walk, and kept it up afterwards—continued, repeated or habitual action. Had this man only leaped once and walked once, after having stood up on his feet, this fact would have been clearly recorded here by the use of the Aorist tense (hēlato and periepatēse). The use of the Imperfect tense, however, tells us, as clearly as language can express it, that the leaping and the walking was a continued, repeated and habitual thing from that time on.

But, asks some sincere seeker after truth, suppose on the day of Pentecost, and in Acts 10:44 and Acts 19:6 they had continued speaking with tongues for two or three hours continuously and then had stopped to never again so speak, would not such continuous speaking have required the use of the Imperfect tense? No. If the speaking with tongues had only occured that once and then ceased forever, no matter if the speaking had lasted for hours, it would have been expressed by the Aorist tense. We are sure of this from such a passage as Luke 23:44: "And it was about the sixth hour [noon], and there was darkness over all the

25

earth until the ninth hour [3 P. M.]." This darkness therefore lasted three full hours. Now what tense expresses this three hours of continuous darkness, the Aorist or the Imperfect? Luke 23:44, "......and there was ["egeneto"—third singular, 2 Aorist of "ginomai"] darkness over all the earth until the ninth hour. (45) And the sun was darkened [eskotisthē— third singular, 1 Aorist passive of "skotizō"] and the veil of the temple was rent [eschisthē—third singular, 1 Aorist passive of "schizō," I split] in the midst." Note, the darkness continued three continuous hours, while the veil of the temple was rent in a moment, yet both events are expressed by the Aorist tense, because they only happened on this one occasion, and were never repeated. Had one of these events been repeated again and again on subsequent occasions, the Imperfect tense and not the Aorist would have been used.

Another honest seeker after truth here asks, Why then is the Aorist tense used in both Acts 2:4 and Acts 4:31? Acts 2:4, "And they were all filled [eplēsthēsan—1 Aorist passive of pimplēmi] with the Holy Ghost, etc." Acts 4:31, "And when they had prayed.....they were all filled [eplēsthēsan—1 Aorist passive of pimplēmi] with the Holy Ghost." Since this experience of being filled with the Holy Ghost was here repeated, why was not the Imperfect tense used in Acts 2:4 instead of the Aorist? Because in Acts 2:4 only the 120 were filled. In Acts 4:31 those filled were the new converts of Acts 2:41, where 3,000 were saved, and of Acts 4:4, where 5,000 more were saved. We draw this conclusion from Acts 4:23, where we read, "And being let go they went to their own company." This reads literally, "they went to their own" (tous idious). The word "company" is not in the Greek text. This expression "tous idious" (their own) includes all Christ's true followers then in Jerusalem. We know this from Acts 4:29, where the very same persons are called "the servants," or "the bond-servants" (tois doulois) of Christ. The vast majority of these persons, most likely all of them, were here filled for the first time. The use of the Aorist tense in Acts 2:4, Acts 4:31, Acts 9:17, Acts 10:44, Acts 11:15 and Acts 19:6, where persons were first filled with the Holy Ghost, is positive proof that, in God's sight, the baptism or first filling was a different experience in all these lives from any later refilling, and was never exactly repeated.

These hard and fast grammatical rules hold good throughout the whole range of Greek literature, and so when we find in Acts 2:4, Acts 10:44-46 and Acts 19:6, that the words denoting "the baptism" or "the infilling of the Holy Spirit" are always expressed by the Aorist tense, while "the speaking with tongues" is always expressed, as we have clearly shown, by the Imperfect tense, this is positive and absolute proof, (1) that they did not speak with tongues until the filling with the Holy Ghost had become a completed or past action, and (2) that when they did speak with tongues they continued so to do. It was from that time a continual, customary and habitual thing. This is the exact meaning of the Imperfect tense, as we have most clearly shown. In each case, therefore, "the speaking with tongues" was "the gift of tongues"— something continued, repeated, habitual—and not God's sign or seal to them of their baptism. To any Greek scholar this is so evident that there can be no possible room for doubt. Praise God for the Greek language.

Friend, let us remind you again that if you spoke with tongues at the time of your baptism or infilling, and have not done so since, you were not baptized according to Acts 2:4.

Reader, let us here inform you that the word for "tongue" in Acts 2:4 is "glōssa." The first meaning of this word is "the tongue as an organ of the body": the secondary meaning is "a language." In Acts 2:6 and 8 however, the word for language and tongue is the very same; viz., "dialektos," which always means a language. Where this word "dialektos" (language) is used in conjunction with "glōssa," "glōssa" retains its first meaning as an organ of the body nine times out of ten. Then the real miracle of Acts 2:4 was that the Holy Spirit so controlled their tongues that, for the time being, they were all speaking different languages, but with other tongues than their own, because another person (the Holy Spirit) was fully controlling those tongues, using them as His very own.

Chapter 3

Dealing With "Difficulties"

Two Seeming Difficulties Answered

First Difficulty:

"What about Mark 16: 17?" asks some sincere seeker after truth: "And these signs shall follow to them having believed [literal translation]. In my name shall they cast out devils; they shall speak with new tongues."

Please notice that this speaking with new tongues was to be one of the signs (semeion—a visible sign) following to "those having believed" (tois pisteusasin, 1 Aorist participle, Dative case) on the Lord Jesus Christ for salvation, and not to those having been filled with the Spirit. This fact is too frequently overlooked by some people.

The word for "tongue" here is "glōssa" and its first meaning is "an organ of the body." The word for "new" here is "kainos," and means, "new, fresh, anew or renewed" (see Greek Dictionary). Examine its use elsewhere. *Mark 2:21,* "No man also seweth a piece of new [kainos] cloth on an old garment: else the new [kainos] piece that filled it up taketh away from the old," etc. "New" here simply refers to a new or fresh piece of the same kind of material. *In 2 Cor. 5:17* Paul says, that when a man is really saved, "Old things are passed away; behold, all things are become new [kainos]." This does not mean that everything about us actually changes its very nature, and becomes something entirely different; but it does mean, that, for the new Christian, everything is renewed. The sun seems to shine more brightly, the birds sing more sweetly, and everything seems more lovely and beautiful. *In 2 Peter 3:13* and *Rev. 21:1* we read of "a new [kainos] heaven and a new [kainos] earth," clearly meaning a renewed heaven and a renewed earth. In Lamentations 3:23 we read in the Septuagint (Greek Old Testament), that "the mercies of God are new [kainos] every morning." This brings out the true meaning of "kainos"—fresh, new or renewed. The Greek word for "another" is "heteros," and never "kainos" (new or renewed). Then Mark 16:17 is a prediction that when a sinner really accepts Christ by faith, and becomes a new creature, one sure and certain visible sign will follow—he will speak with a new or a renewed tongue.

The owner of a large Minneapolis factory once called us into his office and said, "My head engineer, Geo. G— was converted in your church last Sunday night and he is entirely changed. As you know he was perhaps the worst curser in the whole city. From morning till night he used to curse everybody and everything, and, because of this, I often thought of discharging him. I refrained from so doing only because he is the most efficient engineer I have ever had. But come out and listen to him now. He took us to a concealed place near the engine room, and we heard him singing:

> I've found a Friend, oh, such a Friend!
> He loved me 'ere I knew Him;
> He drew me with the cords of love,
> And thus He bound me to Him.
> And 'round my heart still closely twine
> Those ties which naught can sever;
> For I am His, and He is mine,
> Forever and forever.

He was assuredly speaking with a new or renewed tongue, exactly what Christ predicted would happen "to those having believed," not "to those having been baptized with the Holy Ghost."

Second Difficulty:

Again some sincere seeker after truth asks, What about Acts 10:45 and 46? Here we read that the Jews, who came with Peter to Cornelius' house, were astonished when the Holy Ghost was poured out upon these Romans (Acts 10:46), "For they heard them speak with tongues and magnify God." *Also what about Peter's words in Acts 11:15;* "And as I began to speak, the Holy Ghost fell on them, as on us at the beginning." Does not this look as if "the speaking with tongues" in Acts 2:4, Acts 11:46 and Acts 19:6 was really the sign or seal of their baptism?

31

A close reading of the Greek here reveals the fact, that what really astonished Peter and the Jews who came with him to Cornelius' house most was, not the fact that God had baptized or filled these Romans with the Holy Ghost—a very unexpected event—but that He had let them speak with tongues just as the hundred and twenty Galileans had done on the day of Pentecost, or at the beginning. Now why should this fact have astonished them?

Fully seven years had now elapsed (see Usher's Chronology) since Pentecost, and hundreds of Christians had evidently been baptized with the Holy Spirit without the gift of tongues, as in Acts 4:31. Acts 4:31, "And when they had prayed, the place was shaken where they were assembled together, and they were all filled [eplēsthēsan—third person plural, Aorist passive] with the Holy Ghost, and they spake [elaloun—third person plural, Imperfect tense] the word of God with boldness." The word here for "filled" is the very same identical word that is used in Acts 2:4; viz., "eplēsthēsan." It is also the 1 Aorist tense as in Acts 2:4, and so declares that the filling was completed before they spoke in tongues or prophesied. This proves beyond the possibility of all doubt that "the infilling" was just as complete in Acts 4:31 as in Acts 2:4; but in Acts 2:4, we read, "......and they began to speak with other tongues as the Spirit gave to them to utter forth." Here the word "gave" ("As the Spirit gave to them to utter forth") is "edidou" (Imperfect tense), and so tells us very clearly that the Spirit gave to them to speak forth then in other tongues, and continued so to do, as we have so clearly proven. *In Acts 4:31* however, "They spake the word of God with boldness," after they had all been filled with the Holy Ghost. Here the word "spake" is "elaloun" (Imperfect tense), and so proves to us, that when they were baptized, instead of speaking with other tongues and continuing to do so, these in Acts 4:31 preached the word with boldness, and continued to do so. Their gift therefore, following their infilling, was "the gift of prophecy," while in Acts 2:4 it was "the gift of tongues."

Now the Jewish church leaders despised and hated the Romans so deeply that, when they heard that Peter had preached to the Romans and baptized them as members of the church, they called a church council to reprimand Peter. God knew this would happen, so He was careful to baptize or fill Cornelius and his household with the Holy Spirit, and give them "the gift of tongues," in exactly the same manner as He had done at Pentecost, in order to silence forever all adverse criticism of Peter. If, however, "speaking with tongues" had been the usual thing following all "baptisms" or "infillings" since Pentecost, then the Jews in Cornelius' house would not have been astonished when they heard them speak with tongues, and Peter would not have felt it incumbent upon him to have said: (Acts 11:15) "The Holy Ghost fell on them, as on us at the beginning." Peter evidently referred the members of the Council back to Pentecost because "speaking with tongues" had been an unheard of gift since that occasion.

We have now clearly proven that "the speaking with tongues" at Pentecost, Cæsarea, and at Ephesus was the gift of tongues following the completed baptism, and not the sign or seal to the believer of the baptism. Employing the Imperfect tense in each of these cases where "the speaking with tongues" is mentioned, tells us most assuredly that they not only spoke with tongues at the time of their baptism, but continued to do so— continued, repeated or habitual action. Could anything be plainer?

Paul corroborates this conclusion, when he says (1 Cor. 14:22) "Wherefore tongues are for a sign [semeion—a visible proof], not to them that believe [the Saints], but to them that believe not." Here then is God's own statement that He never meant "the speaking with tongues" to be the sign or the seal to the Christian of his or her baptism with the Holy Ghost.

Just here some earnest soul asks, What about the reference to "speaking with tongues" in 1 Cor. 12:30, and 1 Cor. 14:2, 4, 5, 6, 8, 27, 29, etc., etc.? Do all these passages refer to the very same experience as is recorded in Acts 2:4, Acts 10:46 and Acts 19:6? Yes. We are absolutely sure of this because the very same words are used in all these cases.

In 1 Cor. 12:30 Paul asks, "Do all speak with tongues?" The Greek reads, "Mē [not] pantes [all] glōssais [with tongues] lalousin [speak—third plural present of laleō, I speak]." When this negative "mē" is used in an interrogative sentence, the answer is always, No. If the negative "ou" is used, the answer is always, Yes. Here then the answer is, No. All do not speak with tongues when baptized or filled with the Holy Ghost, Paul declares. *1 Cor. 14:2,* "For he that speaketh in an unknown tongue, etc." This reads,

"Ho [the one] gar [for] lalōn [speaking—Pres. Participle of laleō, I speak] glōssē [with a tongue]." *The word "unknown" is not in the Greek text.*

1 Cor. 14: 5, "I wish that ye all spake with tongues." The Greek reads, "Thelō [I wish] de [but] pantes [all] humas [you] lalein [Infinitive of laleō—I speak] glōssais [with tongues]."

Wherever speaking with a tongue or tongues is mentioned in 1 Cor. 12: 30, or in 1 Cor. 14, it is always expressed by the use of these same two words "laleō" (I speak) and "glōssa" (the tongue).

In Acts 2: 4 we find these same words, "......and began to speak with other tongues." The Greek reads, "kai [and] ērxanto [began] lalein [Pres. Infinitive of laleō, I speak] heterais glōssais [with other tongues]."

Acts 10: 46, "For they heard them speak with tongues." The Greek reads, "ēkouon [they heard—Imperfect third plural of akouō, I hear] gar [for] autōn [them] lalountōn [speaking—Pres. Participle genitive plural of laleō, I speak] glōssais [with tongues]."

Acts 19: 6, "......and they spake with tongues." The Greek reads, "elaloun [they spake—third person plural Imperfect of laleō, I speak] te [and] glōssais [with tongues, Dative plural of glōssa]."

When Paul uses the very same word for speak (laleō), and the very same word for tongue (glōssa) in 1 Cor. 12 and 14 as we find in Acts 2: 4, Acts 10: 46 and Acts 19: 6, we must conclude that he is speaking of the very same experience in each and every case; viz., the gift of tongues. No Greek scholar could possibly draw any other conclusion. Let us beware of all Bible

35

teachers and preachers who try "to add to or take away from" the word of God in order to support some pet theory or teaching. Believe nothing that is not clearly stated in "the Word": take nothing on mere supposition.

Just here let us say that we have known several saints who, at the time of their baptism, did not receive the gift of tongues, who today have that gift; but they all know well that their baptism or infilling really occurred without the speaking with tongues. This was evidently Paul's experience. Read Acts 9:17, where we are told Paul was filled with the Holy Ghost, but there is here no mention of "speaking with tongues." Had Paul then spoken with tongues the Holy Spirit would have recorded it. Later, however, God gave him this gift (1 Cor. 14:18), just as He has done to several of our friends after their baptism.

Chapter 4

Examining Spiritual Experiences

In addition to this one all-convincing and irrefutable grammatical reason [see pp. 13-28] why we know speaking with tongues is not the one and only infallible sign or seal of the baptism with the Holy Ghost, let us here give seven other valid reasons.

(1) *Because Elizabeth was filled with the Holy Ghost and did not speak with tongues.*

Luke 1:41, "And it came to pass when Elizabeth heard the salutation of Mary, the babe leaped in her womb: and Elizabeth was filled [eplēsthē—the same word and the same Aorist tense as Acts 2:4] with the Holy Ghost: (42) And [what? spoke with tongues?

No.] she spake out with a loud voice, and said, Blessed art thou among women," etc. The use of "eplēsthē" (was filled—Aorist tense) proves that her filling was complete to the overflowing point.

(2). *Because Zacharias was baptized or filled with the Holy Ghost, and he did not speak with tongues.*

Luke 1:67, "And his father, Zacharias, was filled [eplēsthē—the same word and the same Aorist tense as Acts 2:4] with the Holy Ghost, and [what? spoke with tongues? No.] and prophesied, saying, (68) Blessed be the Lord God of Israel, etc."

(3) *Again we know all will not speak with tongues when baptized, because our Lord Jesus did not so speak.*

Mark 1:10, "He [Christ] saw the heavens opened, and the Spirit like a dove descending upon him. (11) And there came a voice from heaven, saying, Thou art my beloved Son." In Luke 4:18, Christ tells us what happened at His baptism: "The Spirit of the Lord is upon me because he hath anointed me [baptized me] to preach the gospel." Christ did not speak with tongues.

(4) *When baptized all will not speak with tongues because Joel has predicted that prophecy (preaching or teaching the gospel) will accompany the baptism of many.*

Joel 2:28, "And it shall come to pass afterward [in last days] that I will pour out my Spirit upon all flesh, and your sons and your daughters shall [what? speak with tongues? No.] prophesy," as the saints did who are mentioned in Acts 4:31. Acts 4:31, "And they were all filled with the Holy Ghost, and they [what? spoke with tongues? No.] spake the word of God with boldness." They prophesied, as Joel predicted, and Joel's prediction will be especially true "in these last days."

(5) *Again we are absolutely sure that all baptized Christians will not speak with tongues, because the most spiritual saints since the Apostolic days have not so spoken when baptized or filled with the Holy Ghost.*

Read the lives of Polycarp, Justin Martyr, Irenaeus, Tertullian, Origen, Augustine, Martin Luther, Savonarola, Madam Guyon, Fenelon, Geo. Fox, John Bunyan, John Wesley, Chas. Wesley, Whitefield, Fletcher, Christmas Evans, Lorenzo Dow, Peter Cartwright, Jonathan Edwards, Billy Bray, David Brainerd, A. B. Earle, Murray McCheyne, E. P. Hammond, John G. Paton, Chas. H. Spurgeon, Geo. Muller, A. J. Gordon, Andrew Murray, Hudson Taylor, D. L. Moody, General Booth, Wilbur Chapman, A. B. Simpson, A. T. Pierson, Evan Roberts, F. B. Meyer, John McNeil, and Stuart Holden, and you will find that none of these spoke with tongues when baptized. Read Lawson's, "Deeper Experiences of Famous Christians."

In Mr. Lawson's book (p. 308) we have recorded A. B. Earle's account of his own baptism. He says, "I felt that I must have in my heart something that I did not possess......I was in my room alone, pleading for the fullness of Christ's love, when all at once a sweet, heavenly peace filled all the vacuum of my soul, leaving no longing, no unrest, no dissatisfied feeing in my bosom. I felt, I knew that I was accepted fully in Jesus. A calm, simple, childlike trust took possession of my whole being.

39

"Then, for the first time in my life, I had the rest which is more than peace.......

"This change occurred about five o'clock, on the evening of the second day of November, 1863; and although I never felt so weak and small, yet Jesus has been my all since then. There has not been one hour of conscious doubt or darkness since that time."

From that time, we learn from Mr. Earle's great book, "Bringing in the Sheaves," he experienced wonderful spiritual power in all his meetings, and thousands were won to Christ: but he did not speak with tongues.

We once heard Dr. F. B. Meyer give his experience in his own church in London. He was hungry for the deeper things of God, so he went to the Keswick convention. Here he heard Spirit-filled men tell how God had blessed them. Dr. Meyer then began to pray much and earnestly that God would fill him. One night, after earnest prayer, he went to bed and had a vision. He saw the Lord Jesus come to him, and say, "My son, will you give me every key to every door of your heart?" He says, "I saw myself handing a ring of keys to my Lord. He looked keenly into my face and asked, 'My son, are they all here?'" Mr. Meyer replied, "All but one little key to a very small room in my heart." This was some one little habit he was not quite ready to yield up. The Saviour looked very sad and said, "I must have them all or I will take none at all"; and He vanished. Dr. Meyer then awoke, leaped out of bed, dropped upon his knees, and cried, "Here, Lord, is the last and only key. I surrender all to Thee from this moment." Then, he tells us, the glory of the Lord fairly surged into his heart, and from that moment Christ became more real to him than his wife or dear ones. He then knew what it meant to stand in the very presence of God. From that time too, the gift of prophecy was given to him and his world-wide ministry of preaching and teaching really began. Now Dr. Meyer's experience has been the experience of nearly all these famous Christians above mentioned. They did not speak with tongues, and yet they were just as truly filled with the Holy Ghost as any saint who has spoken with tongues. Their lives have proven this fact.

"But God's method of baptizing His saints has changed in these last days," says some sincere tongue advocate.

We must all admit—if we have honestly investigated the matter—that more and more of God's saints are receiving this gift of tongues when baptized. Why is this? Because Pentecost was only a sample of what God promised to do in the last days. Acts 2:16, "And it shall come to pass in the last days, saith God, I will pour out of my Spirit upon all flesh; and your sons and your daughters shall prophesy," etc. Every time we see God pouring out His Spirit, and then giving this gift of tongues, as at Pentecost, it ought to vividly remind us that the last days are upon us, and Christ will soon be coming again.

But just here remember two great facts:

(a) *That the speaking with tongues at Pentecost was the gift of tongues and not the sign or seal of the baptism.* They spake (Acts 2:4), "as the Spirit gave [edidou—third person singular, Imperfect tense] to them to utter forth." As we have very clearly proven

41

(see pp. 13-28) the Imperfect tense here assures us that they spoke with tongues then and continued to do so, for the Imperfect tense in Greek always denotes something continued, repeated or habitual. This fact removes all doubt, and makes us absolutely sure that the speaking with tongues at Pentecost was the gift of tongues and not the sign or seal of the baptism.

(b) *Again remember here that God is unchangeable in His nature and in His mode of action.*

Malachi 3:6, "I am the Lord, I change not."

James 1:17, "With whom [God] is no variableness neither shadow of turning." This clearly teaches that God does not change in the slightest degree. *Hebrews 13:8,* "Jesus Christ [God] the same yesterday, and to-day, and forever."

Now since God is unchangeable and without variableness, even though He is today pouring out His Spirit as in Apostolic days, and giving again the gift of tongues to many, He must also continue to baptize many others just as He baptized those saints in *Acts 4:31,* and as He has baptized nearly all His saints since; viz., without this gift of tongues. He must do this to be true to His own word. *Malachi 3:6,* "I am the Lord, I change not."

To have the blessed Holy Spirit actually take possession of our tongue, and use it Himself to praise and glorify the Lord Jesus Christ, is an experience to be greatly desired by us all, but Paul assures us that there is something much more desirable than this. Read *1 Cor. 14:5,* "I would that ye all spake with tongues, but rather [mallon—very much more] that ye prophesied." Yes, Paul says the gift of prophesy is much more to be longed for than the gift of tongues. Is Paul a reliable authority on this subject?

(6) *A sixth reason why we know that speaking with tongues is not the one and only sign or seal of the baptism with the Holy Ghost, is because Satan can readily counterfeit this sign.*

(a) *He does it constantly today in Spiritualistic meetings.* An old friend of ours, now a Spiritualistic leader, tells us that people often both speak with other tongues and sing with other tongues in his meetings. Since this is true, do you suppose that God would make "speaking with tongues" the one and only sign of the baptism? Never. This would be unthinkable.

(b) *Again Satan often enters Christian assemblies and causes genuine saints to speak with tongues, whenever they are seeking tongues rather than the Holy Ghost Himself.*

A Spirit-filled friend of ours attended an Assembly in a certain Canadian city in company with a Chinese missionary. They heard a splendid Gospel message, and then remained to pray. During the prayer service a good sister began to speak with tongues. It was a genuine tongue all right, but there was something so harsh and repelling, and the woman's face was such a picture of misery and agony, that our friend knew instinctively that it was not of God. Then the missionary whispered to him and said, "She is speaking Chinese, the very dialect I have been preaching in for 20 years, and she is blaspheming the Lord Jesus Christ in a most awful manner." He then interpreted the awful language to our friend, who in turn told us regarding it. Now that dear woman was a real child of God, and her pastor and the saints supposed she was receiving a wonderful baptism with the Holy Ghost. The trouble was she was seeking a manifestation rather than the Holy Spirit Himself. This always grieves the Holy Ghost, and so gives Satan a chance to do his deceptive work even in Christian assemblies.

Our own experience in this matter leads us to the conclusion that, wherever people really believe they must speak with tongues to be baptized with the Holy Ghost, a large percentage of all such either speak a mere "gibberish," or a real language, which, however, the Holy Spirit has nothing whatever to do with.

But praise God there is one sign the Devil cannot possibly counterfeit. It is the genuine Christian love of 1 Cor. 13:1, "Though I speak with the tongues of men and of angels [all the languages spoken in earth and heaven] and have not love, I am become as a sounding brass, or a tinkling cymbal." John assures us that this love ("agapē") can only come from God. 1 John 4:7, "Beloved, let us love one another: for love ["agapē"] is of God; and every one that loveth is born of God, and knoweth God." Most assuredly in Paul's estimation the real test of whether or not we are baptized or filled with the Holy Ghost, is the manifestation of the Spirit's fruit in our daily living, and the first fruit is the love of 1 Cor. 13. See Gal. 5:22 regarding the fruit of the Spirit.

(7) *A seventh reason why we know all persons baptized with the Holy Spirit will not speak with tongues, is because of our own experience.* We would not here mention this, only we feel it might be helpful to others.

When praying earnestly one night (Nov. 21, 1922), the blessed Holy Spirit came down upon us. We saw a light, far brighter than the noon-day sun—a perfect blaze of glory. Then hundreds of tongues of fire seemed to dart forth upon and about us. Then for an hour or more great billows of glory, indescribably beautiful from the standpoint of light and colors, began to roll through our soul like mighty breakers over a sandy beach. Did any outsider need to tell us that the Holy Spirit had entered our life in a new way? No, indeed. Then the blessed Spirit took possession of our tongue, and for an hour or more made us praise the Lord Jesus in a way we had never praised Him before. We were literally speaking with another tongue as the Spirit gave to us to utter forth, but it was all in English.

Some of the hundred and twenty Galileans on the day of Pentecost had our very experience. Twice in our life we have actually heard the voice of God and His very words. One Monday morning in Minneapolis we were rushing for a street car to go to a minister's meeting, when a voice said, "Go back and get your Greek Testament." We got it, and oh, how we praised God, for by means of that Testament we were able that morning to utterly demolish the arguments of a certain good brother against the Virgin Birth of our Lord.

The second time was in Duluth. About four o'clock one morning we were suddenly awakened out of a sound sleep, when a voice said to us, "Did you notice last night, when you read Acts 2, that one of the peoples which heard their very own [idios] language [dialektos] spoken on the day of Pentecost, was the inhabitants of Judea?" We praised God for calling our attention to this fact, for we knew that the Gali-

45

leans (the whole hundred and twenty were Galileans, (Acts 2:7) and the Judeans spoke the very same language in Christ's day; viz., the Aramaic, called Hebrew in the New Testament.

Schaff-Herzog's Encyclopedia (Vol. I, p. 125): "After the exile the Aramaic gradually became the popular language of Palestine, not only of Galilee and Samaria, *but also of Judea. Christ and the Apostles spoke it.*" Here then we have positive proof that some of the hundred and twenty Galileans, after having been filled with the Holy Ghost, praised God in their very own language, but they did it only as the Holy Spirit gave to them to utter forth. The Holy Spirit was running their tongues just as completely as He was running the tongues of those other Galileans speaking some foreign language. *Now since the Holy Spirit made some of the one hundred and twenty Galileans praise the Lord in their very own tongue, we ought to expect that He will cause some of His saints to do the same today.* Ten thousand sincere saints might tell us that we were not baptized or filled on the above occasion because we did not praise the Lord in a foreign tongue, but, praise God, we know what He did for us Nov. 21, 1922; and it is written, 1 Cor. 12:7, "But the manifestation is given to each [ekastō] to profit withal."

Now Paul in 1 Cor. 12:30 asks: "Have all the gifts of healing? do all speak with tongues?" The expected answer, as assured by the use of the negative "mē," is, No! *Reader, will you believe Paul, or these many sincere and good men and women, who, through ignorance or the original Greek text, which alone is inspired of God, [see pp. 13-28], are telling you that all must speak with tongues as the one and only infallible sign of being baptized or filled with the Holy Ghost?*

The writer has a very high regard for all the real saints of God who hold and advocate the teaching he is here opposing. Hundreds of them have had a marvelous experience, and the Holy Spirit is using them to win many precious souls. They all love and revere the Bible as God's own inspired word, and if they are making any mistakes in their teaching—as we are fully convinced they are—these mistakes are of the head only, and not of the heart. Any one of these dear people, who has had a real, genuine Pentecostal experience (and hundreds of them have had) is worth more to the Lord Jesus Christ than any 100 good orthodox Christians—clergy included—who are not filled with the Holy Ghost.

This accounts for that lilt, joy and holy enthusiasm for souls which today characterizes many Pentecostal young people who have been genuinely filled with the Holy Ghost, and it is this which is today drawing to their assemblies hundreds of young people from other churches. These dear people are unscriptural when they teach that "speaking with tongues" is the only Bible evidence of the baptism with the Holy Ghost, as we have clearly proven; but God is blessing many of their assemblies in a marvelous way and giving them great soul winning power just because they are most earnestly urging all their people to seek this infilling, that they might obtain God's power for service. Most other churches are utterly unconcerned regarding this Holy Ghost power, and are not urging their people to pray earnestly that they might be filled. Wherever there is spiritual lethargy, this is the reason.

47

Reader, without this Holy Ghost power all your efforts for Jesus Christ will accomplish nothing worth while. Why? Because you lack the real power of God in your life. *Acts 1:18*, "But ye shall receive power, after that the Holy Ghost is come upon you: and ye shall be witnesses unto me [you can't help it when He controls you], both in Jerusalem, and in Judea, and in Samaria, and unto the uttermost part of the earth."

Chapter 5

Pondering the Apostles

All Spiritual Problems Dealt With by Paul

In 1 Cor. 12:1, Paul says, "Now concerning spiritual gifts, brethren, I would not have you ignorant." The word "gifts" is not in the Greek text. The Greek reads, "Peri de tōn pneumatikōn" (now concerning the spiritual). The right word to supply in all such cases, where no special neuter noun has as yet been mentioned, is "pragmata" (things). Then Paul's assertion is (1 Cor. 12:1) that he is now going to speak "concerning spiritual things" or all spiritual matters, and not alone regarding spiritual gifts. This fact has been overlooked by those who draw a distinction between "the gift of tongues" and "speaking with tongues."

Paul says (1 Cor. 12:7), "But the manifestation of the Spirit is given to every man [ekastō—to each one] to profit withal." *Note*, "the manifestation [hē phanerōsis—the showing forth] of the Spirit is given to each person individually [ekastō], to profit withal." This manifestation then is for each individual's own benefit, and not for the benefit of any one else.

In Rom. 8:6 we read, "The Spirit himself beareth witness with our spirit that we are the children of God." If the Holy Spirit can so witness with our spirits, when we are regenerated, cannot He give us each an inward manifestation when He baptizes or fills us? This is exactly what Paul asserts He will do. 1 Cor. 12:7, "But the manifestation is given to each individual (ekastō) for that individual's own profit." Then, praise God, we are not dependent upon any outward manifestation to be assured of our baptism or infilling. 1 Jno. 5:6, "And it is the Spirit that beareth witness, because the Spirit is truth." Yes, when the Spirit baptizes us He will most assuredly manifest Himself, and we will know it just as certainly as the Saints who were filled in Acts 2:4; *and when the Holy Spirit does manifest or show forth Himself to each one individually, at least four things will follow:*

(1) *He will cause us to praise the Lord Jesus Christ as never before in all our lives.*

Jno. 16:13, "Howbeit when he, the Spirit of truth, is come...... (14) He shall glorify me." The Spirit's business being to glorify Jesus Christ, He will most assuredly cause us to praise the Lord when He controls our lives.

(2) *He will make Christ real to us.* We will verily

feel His presence, and live in that very presence.

Jno. 14:18, "I will not leave you comfortless [orphanous—orphans] I will come to you." Yes, He comes to us in the person of the Holy Ghost. The Spirit will then cause us to realize that we are a part of Christ's own body; that He is the vine and we are one of the branches drawing our life, our sustenance, and our strength from Him.

(3) *When baptized or filled with the Holy Ghost, each person will manifest forth the fruit of the Spirit in his or her daily life.*

Gal. 5:22, "But the fruit of the Spirit is love, joy, peace, longsuffering, gentleness, goodness, faith, (23) Meekness, temperance [self-control]." When the Holy Ghost is controlling us in thought, word and act— the indisputable manifestation of His presence to others —then His fruit will grow on the tree of our lives as naturally as apples grow on the apple tree. Paul rivets this truth home by saying (1 Cor. 13:1), "Though I speak with the tongues of men and of angels [all the tongues spoken on earth and in heaven] and have not *love* [the first fruit of the Spirit], I am become [literally—I have become] as sounding brass, or a tinkling cymbal."

Beloved, are we Spirit-filled? If so we are controlled by love, the love of 1 Cor. 13. Read 1 Cor. 13: 4-8 and find out just where we stand. 1 Cor. 13:4, "Love suffereth long, and is kind; love envieth not; love vaunteth not itself, is not puffed up, (5) Doth not behave itself unseemly, seeketh not her own, is not easily provoked, thinketh no evil; (6) Rejoiceth not in iniquity, but rejoiceth in the truth; (7) Beareth all things [insults, injuries, harsh and unjust treatment], believeth all things [not suspicious of others], hopeth all things [always optimistic], endureth all things. (8) Love never faileth." If we have this love (the first fruit of the Spirit) controlling us in thought, word and conduct, we are baptized with the Holy Ghost: if this love is not controlling us in thought, word and conduct we are not baptized or filled with the Holy Ghost, no matter what manifestations or experiences we may have had. We were either mistaken in the first place, or we have grieved the blessed Spirit, and He has ceased to control us as before.

(4) *Again when the Holy Ghost baptizes or fills us, each of us will be given at least one spiritual gift.*

1 Cor. 12:7, "For the manifestation is given to each one [ekastō] to profit withal. (8) For to one is given by the Spirit:

1. "The word of wisdom.
2. "To another the word of knowledge, by the same Spirit.
3. "To another faith by the same Spirit.
4. "To another the gifts of healing by the same Spirit.
5. "To another the working of miracles.
6. "To another prophecy.
7. "To another discerning of spirits.
8. "To another divers kinds of tongues.
9. "To another the interpretation of tongues."

1 Cor. 12:11, "But all these worketh that one and the same Spirit dividing to each one [ekastō] separately as he wills. (29) Are all apostles? are all prophets?

are all teachers? are all workers of miracles? (30) Have all the gifts of healing? do all speak with tongues? do all interpret?" The evident answer is, No! *But Paul clearly implies here that at least one gift will be given to each person, when the Holy Ghost manifests Himself in their lives, or baptizes them.*

Peter teaches this same truth very clearly in 1 Peter 4:10, *"As every man [ekastos—each] hath received a gift [not the gift], even so minister the same one to another, as good stewards of the manifold grace of God."* The word for gift here is "charisma," the very same word that we find in 1 Cor. 12:4. Yes, when the Holy Spirit manifests Himself, as promised in 1 Cor. 12:7, He gives to each person at least one gift.

Chapter 6

Concluding Advice

1. *To the scores of dear brethren who are bitterly opposed to speaking with tongues.* Listen to Paul's words. 1 Cor. 14:39, "Wherefore, brethren, covet to prophesy, and forbid not to speak with tongues."

a. *All will in reality be forbidding others to speak with tongues,* who declare most emphatically that there is no genuine speaking with tongues today. From our own experience already narrated, and from the experiences of many other reliable witnesses, we know that speaking with genuine tongues today is a great reality. Instead of opposing this gift of tongues, we ought to praise God for again bringing this gift back to His church.

b. *Again all will forbid others to speak with tongues who declare,* as hundreds do today, that all speaking with tongues is of the devil.

1 Cor. 12:10 informs us that "speaking with tongues" is one of the gifts of the Holy Ghost. Now the Holy Spirit is here today with all the power and authority which He had in the Apostolic days. See 1 Thess. 1:5 and Rom. 15:19. Why then should not all His gifts be in the church today?

Many dear saints have the gift of tongues today. We have heard some of them pray in a foreign tongue, when God has put some great burden on their hearts for lost and perishing souls. As the Holy Spirit pleaded through them, you detected the very presence and power of God. Oh, what heart-thrilling appeals were those. You felt, as you listened, a spirit of awe, and you realized the very presence of God. We have known such saints, after being on their faces before God for an hour or more pouring forth their petitions (or letting the Holy Ghost pour forth His petitions through them), to be unable to speak English for another hour or so.

Brother, this gift of tongues has come back to the church, and will be more and more prevalent until Jesus comes. If you say this is all of Satan, you will surely offend the Holy Ghost, and He may forsake you, and leave you as powerless as He has left many others.

Friend, we had better obey Paul's word and "Forbid not to speak with tongues." Let us take "the middle of the road attitude" on this subject. Let us realize that this gift has come back to the church, and if God should give some saint a message in tongues in your congregation—and He might

—let him deliver it without interruption, but pray God to give the interpretation to some one. If, after the message has been delivered, there is no interpreter present, then remember Paul's words (1 Cor. 14:28), "But if there be no interpreter, let him keep silence in the church; and let him speak to himself, and to God."

Sometime some one may speak with tongues in your meeting, and you will feel at once that it is not of God. It will be harsh and repelling; your spiritual nature will revolt. Then just quietly place your hand upon such an one and ask God to rebuke the evil spirit, and you will have very little trouble. By this mode of procedure you will keep out all fanaticism, and yet you will not interfere with the genuine working of the Holy Ghost; for never forget that the gift of tongues is back in the church today. If ever God needed wise and firm spiritual leaders it is now.

II. *Words of advice to the hungry saints who are seeking the baptism or infilling with the Holy Ghost.*

1. *Don't agonize to be baptized.*

Christ told His disciples (Luke 24:49) "......tarry ye in the city of Jerusalem, until ye be endued with power from on high." The word for "tarry" here is "kathisate," the 1 Aorist Imperative, second person plural of "kathizō," I sit down. Then Christ's command was to just sit down and wait in Jerusalem, fully expecting Him to do what He had promised to do not many days hence (Acts 1:5).

Then in Acts 2:2 we read, "And suddenly there came a sound from heaven as of a mighty rushing wind, and it filled all the house where they were sitting."

The Greek word here for "sitting" is "kathēmenoi," the Present participle of "kathēmai"—I sit down. *However, these 120 disciples spent most of their time in prayer* until they knew everything in their lives was completely surrendered to God; until absolutely nothing remained between themselves and God. *We are certain of this from Acts 1:14,* where we read, "These all were steadfastly continuing with one accord in prayer and supplication." Literally this reads, "These all were [ēsan—Imperfect tense] persistently continuing [proskarterountes—Present participle] with one accord in prayer [proseuchē] and supplication [deēsei]," etc. The use of the Imperfect tense here (ēsan—continued, repeated or habitual past action) coupled with the Present participle of the verb proskartereō (I persistently continue), is positive assurance that earnest, supplicating prayer was their chief and principal occupation during those ten days of waiting. This is always essential ere the Holy Spirit will baptize any saint. Then, between times, they would just sit there and talk to each other about Jesus, living the past over again, recalling many of His marvelous teachings, which now —after His resurrection and ascension—they could for the first time comprehend. The very atmosphere was impregnated with the name of Jesus; from morning until night He was in their thoughts, the topic of all their conversation. How they would praise and thank Him for His redeeming love and for the promise of the Holy Ghost, who was so soon to fall upon them and give them real power for service.

Why not today hold conventions or Tarry-Meetings, like that first Tarry-Meeting in Jerusalem, where all

58

will attend who really want to be baptized or filled with the Holy Ghost? For a few days, or a week, just lay all else aside and meet to think about the Lord Jesus, to pray to Him as the 120 did, to sing about Him, to talk about Him, but chiefly to praise and thank Him for His redeeming love. Such a convention or Tarry-Meeting would only draw earnest, hungry souls, but oh, how God would bless and fill all hungry hearts.

Dr. A. B. Simpson evidently had some such thought as this in his mind, when he wrote that splendid hymn, "Tarry for the Power" (Hyms of the Christian Life, p. 80). The first of five verses reads:

> We are waiting for the Promise of the Father,
>   We are seeking while the Lord is nigh;
> He has bidden us to tarry for the blessing;
>   We are waiting for the power from on high.

Chorus

> Tarry for the power from on high:
>   Come while the Lord is nigh;
> Wait for the Promise of the Father,
>   Tarry, tarry for the power from on high.

Remember, this gift of the Holy Ghost is for all Christians today, just as much as for the Disciples. Acts 2:39, "For the promise is unto you and to your children, and to all that are afar off, even to as many as the Lord our God shall call." "Proskalesētai [shall call] is the 1 Aorist Subj. Middle voice of "proskaleō," I call forth, and so really means, as many as the Lord our God may have called or saved. This means that this gift is for each of us today, who really loves God.

Being assured this gift is for us, then let us:

a. *Pray earnestly until we know that God has cleansed our hearts and removed every obstruction, thus enabling us to make a 100% consecration* to Him. Beloved, there must be a genuine willingness and longing to be emptied before the Holy Ghost can fill us; and no heart has ever yet received this longing, but as the result of earnest prayer.

b. *Having prayed, then, like the Disciples, let us spend our time thinking of our blessed Lord, praising and adoring Him.* Then ask Him to engender the necessary faith in our hearts to receive the Holy Ghost. In the last analysis we must all receive the Holy Ghost by faith. Galatians 3:14, ".....that we might receive the promise of the Spirit through faith."

2. *Second word of advice to hungry seekers:*

Just seek the infilling of the Holy Ghost, and let Him manifest Himself as He will.

A Christian Alliance missionary told us that three of his women workers were filled with the Holy Ghost about the same time. Being hungry for all God had, they had been spending much time in prayer, and this gift only comes through prayer, purity and praise. They just lived for days in His presence. Then God filled one of them, and gave her the gift of tongues. The second was filled and God gave her a baptism of love. The third one was filled, and for days there seemed to be a veritable fire burning within her. The final results, said the missionary, were the same in each of the three cases. At once the fruit of the Spirit was manifest in each life. Each received a burning love for lost souls, and began to make opportunities to get into homes where they knew they were not wanted.

Then too, Christ became very real to each of them, and they knew what it meant to really walk and talk with Him: yet the Spirit's manifestation to each one was different.

3. Third word of advice.

When seeking the infilling of the Holy Ghost do not stop short of a real and genuine inward (not outward) experience. When the Holy Spirit really fills us we will know it. He will manifest His presence to one in one way and to another in another; but there will be a manifestation to each for that person's benefit (1 Cor. 12:7).

We meet so many people whose pastors have told them to take the Holy Ghost by faith, and they did so to the best of their ability, but there was no change in their lives; the glory of the Lord never surged through their souls, Christ was not made real to them, and there has been no manifestation as promised by Paul in 1 Cor. 12:7: "But the manifestation [phanerōsis—showing forth] of the Spirit is given to every man ["ekastō"—to each] to profit withal." In other words they received nothing at all. Why? Because their hearts were not prepared first by waiting upon God in earnest prayer. *If pastors do not encourage their people to meet and pray for this deeper experience until a real hunger is created within the heart, it will be utterly useless to urge them to take the Holy Ghost by faith.*

Reader, if you want to be filled, you must first let God empty you, or make you willing to be emptied of your pride, selfishness, critical spirit, worldliness, touchiness, stinginess, impurity, and every other unholy and doubtful thing. But God can only do this as you spend hours with Him in prayer. Give God a chance and He will show you just why you have not been baptized or filled, and when your heart is ready, praise His name, He will engender the needful faith, and you will be filled and know it, and others will know it by the transformation in your life. It will then be your highest ambition to live according to 1 Cor. 13.

When you know He has come and filled you, then let no one rob you of your blessing by persuading you that you are not filled because you did not have the very same experience they enjoyed. Scores of people will say, "Did you speak with tongues?" If you say, "No," then they will try to convince you that you were never baptized or filled.

At such times remember: (1) That "the speaking with tongues" at Pentecost, Cæsarea, and Ephesus was the gift of tongues," as we have so clearly proven, (pp. 13-28), something they were able to repeat over and over again, and not the sign or seal of the infilling or baptism. (2) That Paul asserts very clearly, that the supreme test, as regards whether or not we have been filled with the Holy Ghost, is the manifestation of true love in our lives. 1 Cor. 13:1, "Though I speak with the tongues of men and of angels, and have not love, I am become as sounding brass, or a tinkling cymbal." *Once again, what is the nature of this love, of which Paul speaks?* 1 Cor. 13:4, "Love suffereth long, and is kind; love envieth not; love vaunteth not itself, is not puffed up. (5) Doth not behave itself unseemly, seeketh not her own; is not easily provoked, thinketh no evil: (6) Rejoiceth not in iniquity, but rejoiceth in the truth; (7) Beareth all things, believeth all things, hopeth all things, endureth all things. (8) Love never faileth."

Friend, have you this kind of love controlling you in thought, word and deed? If so, you are filled with the Holy Ghost; but if not, you have a very good reason to doubt your baptism or infilling though you once spoke with tongues and had a wonderful manifestation.

A woman told her pastor one evening about her wonderful baptism, and how she spoke with tongues and had a marvelous manifestation. The next day that pastor told this woman's relative regarding it. The relative then informed him that some months before they had quarreled, and had not spoken since. She then requested him to see this woman, who had just been filled with the Holy Spirit, and ask her to come and see her, that they might be friends again. He did so and conveyed the message. She replied, "See her! Well I guess not." Then she said many mean, harsh, unkind things about the other woman. That pastor knew from this that her heart was full of hatred, and that she really had no Holy Ghost love. 1 Cor. 13:4, "Love suffereth long, and is kind; love envieth not ...... (5) Doth not behave itself unseemly, seeketh not her own, is not easily provoked, thinketh no evil," etc., etc. She had spoken with tongues, but most assuredly she had not been baptized with the Holy Ghost.

Again remember that speaking with tongues is almost as common in Spiritualistic and Mormon meetings as in Pentecostal meetings, so we must never forget

Paul's one infallible test by which we can always tell whether the speaking with tongues is of God or of the adversary. 1 Cor. 13:1, "Though I speak with the tongues of men and of angels, and have not love, I am become as sounding brass, or a tinkling cymbal."

Then the supreme test of a Spirit-filled life is the manifestation of love (1 Cor. 13:3-8) in our daily living, for this love is the first fruit of the Spirit. Galatians 5:22, "But the fruit of the Spirit is love, joy, peace, longsuffering, gentleness, goodness, faith, (23) Meekness, temperance [self-control]."

4. *Last word of advice. When baptized or filled with the Holy Spirit, do not think you have all that God has for you.* Remember Paul's words in Eph. 3:20, "Now unto Him that is able to do exceeding abundantly above that we ask or think, according to the power [dunamis—Holy Ghost power: see Luke 24:49 and Acts 1:8] that worketh in us," etc. This simply means that we have no idea what God can and will yet do through each of us if only our mind, heart and will are completely surrendered to the Holy Ghost. Unless, however, we keep constantly remembering this fact after we are first filled with the Holy Spirit, we will either grow indifferent, or we will become spiritually proud; and spiritual pride always spells failure in the service of our Lord.

Beloved, seek the baptism of the Holy Ghost. Christ calls this gift "the promise of the Father." Luke 24:49, "And, behold, I send the promise [tēn epaggelian] of my Father upon you." All other promises are mere promises, but this is "the" promise, because it is the very greatest and most precious gift Christ has to bestow upon His children. So important did Christ consider this gift that He commanded His disciples to tarry in Jerusalem until they received it. Without this Holy Ghost power He knew that all their efforts for Him would be futile. *Why, it was through this Holy Ghost power that the Lord Jesus did all His own mighty works:*

a. *Christ conquered Satan through the power of the Holy Ghost.* Luke 4:1, "And Jesus being full of the Holy Ghost returned from Jordan and was led by the Spirit into the wilderness, (2) Being forty days tempted of the devil."

b. *Christ taught and preached in the power of the Holy Ghost.* Luke 4:14, "And Jesus returned in the power of the Spirit into Galilee:...... (15) And he taught in their synagogues."

c. *Christ did all His work by means of the Holy Ghost.* Luke 4:18, "The Spirit of the Lord is upon me, because he hath anointed me to preach the gospel to the poor; he [the Holy Ghost] hath sent me to heal the broken hearted, to preach deliverance to the captives, and recovering of sight to the blind, to set at liberty them that are bruised."

Acts 10:38 tells us the same great truth: "God anointed Jesus of Nazareth with the Holy Ghost and with power; who went about doing good, and healing all who were oppressed of the devil." Yes, all of Christ's work was done through the power of the Holy Ghost, the Third Person of the blessed Trinity, and not through His own power. Now this Holy Ghost power with which Jesus was anointed (Acts 10:38) is the very same with which He (Jesus) desires to anoint us, because the same word for power is used in both Acts

10:38 and Acts 1:8, where we read, "But ye shall receive power [dunamis], after that the Holy Ghost is come upon you."

Reader, if the Lord Jesus needed the power of the Holy Ghost, how much more do we? No wonder we read (Eph. 5:18), "Be filled with the Spirit."

Praise God this gift is for us today. Acts 2:39, "For the promise is unto you, to your children, and to all that are afar off, even as many as the Lord our God shall call." Has He called you? Yes. Then the promise of the Father, or the gift of the Holy Ghost is for you. Obtain it then by all means, and let God use you to the fullest possible extent.

In praying for the baptism of the Holy Spirit, always pray to the Lord Jesus Christ, for it is His prerogative to baptize with the Holy Ghost. (Mat. 3:11), "He [Christ] shall baptize you with the Holy Ghost and with fire." See also Mk. 1:8, Lu. 3:16, Jno. 1:33 and Lu. 24:49. All these passages tell us that Christ is the baptizer with the Holy Ghost, and not the Holy Ghost Himself.

Let us obey three passages of Scripture and every one of us will most assuredly be baptized with the Holy Ghost:

1. 1 John 3:22, "And whatsoever we ask, we receive of him, because we keep his commandments, and do those things that are pleasing in his sight." Fully determine, by the grace and power of God, to make a practice of keeping God's commandments, and doing only what is pleasing in His sight, and you will be filled. *Acts 5:32* proves this statement: "And we are his witnesses of these things; and so is also the Holy Ghost, whom God hath given to them obeying him

[literal translation]."

2. Rom. 14:22, "Happy is he that condemneth not himself in that thing which he alloweth. (23) ......: for whatsoever is not of faith is sin."

Before we can be filled with the Holy Ghost we must resolve that we will do nothing which is even doubtful; only that of which our conscience can fully and heartily approve as being right in the sight of God.

3. Heb. 12:4, "Ye have not yet resisted unto blood striving [wrestling—antagōnizomenoi] against sin."

We must prove to our Lord that we are determined, by His help, to fight Satan to the very death, as it were. If we are at all lenient with ourselves in allowing this or that pleasurable indulgence, when God says, "Better not," we will never be baptized with the Holy Ghost.

Jno. 15:7, "If ye abide in me, and my words abide in you, ye shall ask what ye will, and it shall be done unto you." Note the "if" here.

Dr. J. Stuart Holden has rightly said, "It comes to me that what we need at this time......is a mighty conviction of the sin of not being filled with the Spirit, for because I am not filled with the Spirit I am not representing Christ to the world as I should do. Because I am not filled with the Spirit, out of me there cannot flow 'rivers of living water' to others in a world that is rushing headlong from God to its own destruction."

Acts 1:8, "But ye shall receive power, after that the Holy Ghost is come upon you: and ye shall be witnesses unto me both in Jerusalem, and in all Judea, and in Samaria, and unto the uttermost part of the earth."

Reader, this power is for us. Let us then determine to possess our rights, and live a life of victory and real soul-winning service for our blessed Lord, who has redeemed us at so great a cost.

Other HORIZON HOUSE books you will enjoy

MY GOD CAN DO ANYTHING! by Clarence Shrier is an amazing account of God's healing intervention in one man's life. Some stories are just incredible—this one is true. 96 pages, paper, $1.50.

TALL TALES THAT ARE TRUE by British Columbia Storyteller Arthur H. Townsend. A fascinating collection of crisply written short stories with spiritual applications. "A Million Dollar Bonfire," "The Pig Was Insured" and many others. An excellent gift. 96 pages, paper, $1.50.

VALLEY OF SHADOWS by Jake Plett. When his wife MaryAnn was abducted and murdered near Edmonton, Alberta, Jake and his two small sons went through seven months of agony and distress. It became an odyssey of faith. Very inspiring. 170 pages, paper, $1.95.

CARIBOO COUNTRY SAINTS AND SHENANIGANS by British Columbia Storyteller Arthur H. Townsend. A rollicking revelation of the author's experiences as a pioneer preacher in a rugged part of Canada. A rustic, romantic, authentic account of old-time faith (and fun!). 128 pages, paper, $1.75.

BEYOND THE TANGLED MOUNTAIN by Douglas C. Percy is an authentic African novel by an award-winning Canadian author. From his pen spins a fascinating web of missionary heroism, romance, tension, and tragedy. Douglas Percy is one of the "best" on Africa. First time in paperback. 158 pages, paper, $1.95.

PREACHERS, PRIESTS, AND CRITTERS edited by Eric Mills. An absorbing collection of unusual accounts. The rough-and-tumble speech of camp meetings is presented in a fascinating manner. Chapter titles include "The Flask that Wouldn't Break," "The Widow-Maker Missed Me," "Rotten Egged" and more. 96 pages, paper, $1.50.

CHOCOLATE CAKE AND ONIONS....WITH LOVE by Marilynne E. Foster is a collection of recipes that she has discovered in her own use to be tasty and easy to prepare. The love comes in selected excerpts from various writings on the theme of love. 96 pages, paper, spiral spine, $1.95.

MEN WITH THE HEART OF A VIKING by Douglas C. Percy is the stirring story of "The Shantymen," courageous men and women who have combined faith and fortitude to carry the Gospel to North America's hinterlands. A challenge in commitment. 147 pages, paper, $1.95.

THE TAMING OF MOLLY by Molly Clark is the author's own account of how God came into her life and changed her. A story of spiritual and physical healing, "backsliding," and progress. Humorous, warm, and helpful. 96 pages, paper, $1.50.

THE HAPPEN STANCE by K. Neill Foster describes the spiritual "stance" designed for routing the forces of evil and unleashing the power of God. For those special people who want to see things "happen" in their Christian experience. 159 pages, paper, $1.95.

THE PURSUIT OF GOD by A.W. Tozer is as contemporary as today's newspaper. And A.W. Tozer is as incisive as any writer can be. Tozer fans will welcome this new edition of an inspirational classic. 128 pages, paper, $1.95.

CHARLES BOWEN: "PAUL BUNYAN" OF THE CANADIAN WEST by W. Phillip Keller. Charles Bowen feared neither noose nor submarine. In Keller's unusual true account he survives both to carry the Gospel to Canada's Western frontier. (Originally entitled **Bold Under God**, Moody Press.) 141 pages, paper, $1.95.

THE JANZ TEAM STORY by Leo Janz. Tells the remarkable story of a Canadian evangelistic ministry that touches three continents. More important, it tells why. 111 pages, paper, $1.95.

FIBBER'S FABLES by Richard H. Boytim. The time-honored fables of Aesop retold in a bright, new format. Complete with biblical applications. Great for kids! 96 pages, $1.75.

THAT INCREDIBLE CHRISTIAN by A.W. Tozer. A legend in his time, Tozer delivers penetrating insights and a stinging wallop for today. Now for the first time in mass market format. 137 pages, paper, $1.95.

HELP FOR HUSBANDS (AND WIVES!) edited by Eric Mills comes with a definite masculine appeal, but has loads of help for ladies too. A series of nine unusual accounts that includes contributions from authors Pete Gillquist, Richard H. Harvey and R. Stanley Tam. 92 pages, paper, $1.75.

70 YEARS OF MIRACLES by Richard H. Harvey is the amazing account of the miraculous in the author's own life. Dr. Harvey's impeccable credentials and lifetime of integrity qualify him to write some unusual things. One you won't want to miss! 192 pages, paper, $1.95.

UFOs: SATANIC TERROR by Basil Tyson. Around the world an estimated six UFOs are sighted every hour. Tyson's explanation is both startling and impressive. 116 pages, paper, $1.95.

CRISIS AT 9:25 by Barry Moore is a collection of hard-hitting messages by an international evangelist from London, Canada. Pointed and provocative. 95 pages, paper, $1.75.

TREASURES IN HEAVEN by Beatrice Sundbo is a warm, human look at how the author faced the deaths of four of her family, then her own death. Inspiring and triumphant. 96 pages, paper, $1.75.

DARE TO SHARE by Marney Patterson. Sub-titled "Communicating the Good News" this is an encouraging handbook on relating the Christian faith to others. Affirms that God's Word does not return void and those sharing it (whether from person to person or from the pulpit) should expect results. 122 pages, paper, $1.95.

Ask for these books from your bookseller. Or order them directly from HORIZON HOUSE PUBLISHERS, Box 600, Beaverlodge, Alberta, Canada. Please include 15 cents for postage and handling for each book ordered.

NOTES

NOTES

NOTES

NOTES

NOTES

NOTES

NOTES

NOTES